Carmen Bugan's books include the memoir *Burying the Typewriter: Childhood Under the Eye of the Secret Police* (Picador), which has received international critical praise, the Bread Loaf Conference Bakeless Prize for Nonfiction, and was a finalist in the George Orwell Prize for Political Writing, and the Dayton Literary Peace Prize. Her collections of poems are *Lilies from America: New & Selected Poems*; *Releasing the Porcelain Birds* and *The House of Straw* (all with Shearsman Books), and *Crossing the Carpathians* (Carcanet) Press. She is also the author of a critical study on *Seamus Heaney and East European Poetry in Translation: Poetics of Exile*. Her work has been translated into several languages and she is a regular reviewer for Harvard Review Online. Bugan was awarded a large grant from the Arts Council of England, was a Creative Arts Fellow in Literature at Wolfson College, Oxford University, was a Hawthornden Fellow, the 2018 Helen DeRoy Professor in Honors at the University of Michigan, and is a George Orwell Prize Fellow. She has a doctorate in English literature from Balliol College, Oxford University.

By the Same Author

Poetry and the Language of Oppression:
Essays on Politics and Poetics
Oxford University Press, 2021

Lilies from America: Selected Poems
Shearsman Books, 2019

Releasing the Porcelain Birds: Poems After Surveillance
Shearsman Books, 2016

Sulla Soglia Della Dimenticanza / On the Side of Forgetting
Edizioni Kolibris, 2015

The House of Straw
Shearsman Books, 2014

Seamus Heaney and East European Poetry in Translation:
Poetics of Exile
MHRA / Routledge, 2014

Burying the Typewriter:
Childhood Under the Eye of the Secret Police
Picador (UK)/ Graywolf (USA), 2012

Crossing the Carpathians
Oxford Poets / Carcanet Press, 2004

Carmen Bugan

Time Being

Shearsman Books

First published in the United Kingdom in 2022 by
Shearsman Books Ltd
PO Box 4239
Swindon
SN3 9FN

Shearsman Books Ltd Registered Office
30–31 St. James Place, Mangotsfield, Bristol BS16 9JB
(this address not for correspondence)

www.shearsman.com

ISBN 978-1-84861-803-9

Copyright © Carmen Bugan, 2022

The right of Carmen Bugan to be identified as the author
of this work has been asserted by her in accordance with the
Copyrights, Designs and Patents Act of 1988.
All rights reserved.

Acknowledgements

Many thanks to the following publications, where poems from this collection appeared: *The Irish Times, Literary Matters*, the Poetry Foundation website, *Oxford Magazine*, Oxford University Press Blog, *Big Scream*, the *Residential College Magazine, Paumanok Transitions, MONK Magazine*, and *Corona. Harvard Review Online* published the prose piece 'Stony Brook'.

First of all, I wish to express my profound gratitude to Tony Frazer, my editor and publisher, for bringing this book to the readers. Carl Schmidt and Christopher Ricks read, commented, and encouraged many of these poems and were of great support to me during the Covid-19 pandemic, providing advice, warmth, and wisdom. Many thanks to Oswyn Murray for supplying Homer's wise thought that became the epigraph for the last section of this book. Richard Bronson and the members of the poetry workshop he leads here in Long Island have read and commented on several of the poems in this collection: many thanks. My children, Alisa and Stefano, for whom most of these poems were written, are my inspiration and joy: no word of poetry is born without them.

Contents

PART I

The house of shells	11
A prayer for my children	13
Water ways	14

PART II

For the time being	19
Lockdown	20
Letter from New York	21
Sitting among the tulips	23
Fields	24
April	27
Blue butterfly	28
Language	29
Air and music	30
Morning hours	31
Do not point your gun at a child	32
Stony Brook	33
The arrow of time	35
Laughter	39
She looks in the mirror	40
September	41
Walking among talking leaves	42
This October, winnowing	44
On this day we send our love	46
The pearl	48
Sfintul Neculai	49
Christmas	51
Time being	52
On the 2021 Presidential Inauguration	53
Aero garden	55
Winter cardinal	56

Anniversary of the heart	57
Morning in the garden	58
A promise	60
Waiting for spring	61

PART III

First of March	65
The tree doctor	66
Hawk	67
Nest of songs	68
Daffodils	69
Mourning Dove eggshell	70
Love poem	71
Irenicon	72
First of May	73

PART IV

Change is afoot	77
Pollen rains	78
Conversation with the soul	79
Their first strawberry	81
Whitsun	82
Crossing the Sound	83
Don't lose heart	84
Up North	87
They discovered singing sands	92
Yvoire	94
Gettysburg	95
The hook	96

For Carl and Judith Schmidt

Part I

L'amor che move il sole e l'altre stelle

(the love which moves the sun and the other stars)

—Dante, *Paradiso* XXXIII

The house of shells

I

Egg-shaped stones, peach-coloured
jingle shells, razor clams,
rosy stones, quahog clams,
blue mussels, scallops and whelk.

Our children ran shouting on sand dunes,
the winter wind lifted their words
in the freezing air, blowing them
into the song of upwelling waves.

The newly-rented, empty home.
There, on a sheet of paper, we drew a house.
We sat on the floor and filled in the walls,
windows, and the roof—with glue,
stones, and golden nacreous shells.

Alisa made a little path of blue mussels
from the white road to the door,
Stefano put in the razor clam chimney,
the whelk was the tree in the garden.

II

Our belongings sailed the wintery Atlantic
for more than one month.
Toys, our beds, plates, books,
clothes took forever to arrive.

We slept on air mattresses
feeling homesick. Homesick for what,
we kept asking ourselves?

III

Now and then someone draws a flower
or a little tree in the garden: after all,
spring shows signs of arrival.
Outside the kitchen door,
a cardinal and a few robins hop around.
The cardinal peers inside:
it looks comfortable with me,
as long as I sit still.

January–March 2016

A prayer for my children

On the US Presidential Inauguration 2017

This year, what you learn at school,
sitting at your tiny desks in the sunny room,
is the "lock-down drill". We come from other
countries, you remind me as you recount hiding
in closets, holding your breath, while your teacher
pulled down the blinds: is this a free country,
you ask. I say that these are changed times.

Out there on the campaign trail, the man
who is now president-elect talked of grabbing women,
calling it "locker room talk," used an arsenal of words
you should not know and should not use,
according to the laws of common decency.
Vulgarity and corruption are as old as the world,
your father says, yet this won't hearten our hearths.

*

This year we bought our first house, stripped rooms
to the bare bones of wood, repaired every wall,
sealed all the holes, changed the wiring to make it safe,
put up a brand-new roof, painted it all.
Neighbors came by to meet us.
We planted our first rose bushes, our first tree.
I won't renounce the hope that you grow your roots.
The world within must meet the world without,
and nothing but love will come out of my pen;
our prayers must join the prayers from others
while the ship of state sails these troubled waters.

Water ways

For Alisa, who shouted, "Mommy, I keep losing your steps!"

The water is writing on sand
many drafts of the same story,

one more shimmering than the next.
I go there to memorize their turns

and feel their calling power,
wrestle with their yesses and whys,

I get involved, make footnotes on some pages;
the ocean erases them impatiently

offering shells the size of my feet,
shhh, it says, now listen.

*

My daughter says the clouds try to bloom
above the water—white hydrangeas—

but the water pulls them down;
clouds are children of the water, I say,

it's hard to let go of children.
Under the bridge this morning the river

passes for a mirror half fogged over—
visions and revisions touch its surface

as we look on; mommy, my child says,
the clouds caress the water.

A white hawk appears above us
held up by the warm breath of the earth,

the tips of its wings recall silver lining
gliding out of view like a thought hard to hold.

Part II

Nel mezzo del cammin di nostra vita

(In the middle of our life's journey)

—Dante, *Inferno*, Canto I, line 1

For the time being

We are fine, they say, for the time being.
Enough food in the pantry, prescriptions filled,
No need to go out of the house,
Except to let the dog run in the yard.

Our road has fallen silent, we can hear the trees
Near the river, it feels like a long Sunday
But without the church. There is plenty of time
To watch the trees bloom. When was the last time?

The elderly are used to sitting the days.
But we are also fine, the younger ones, for the time
Being. We have time to play with our children,
Bake, wash the curtains, and make love again, finally!

Now that the shelves at the shops are empty
And the parking lots are drive-through
Testing labs, we have time to pray
For those who are dying in the hospitals.

We pray the nurses will stay healthy through
Extended working shifts. We pray the doctors
Get a good night sleep before they fight to grip life
Slipping through their hands, for the time being.

In other countries many sing from their balconies
To cheer each other up through so much dying,
We call, check in, reassure, and smile
From a distance, hoping: for the time being.

Lockdown

children are
flowering
at the windows

Letter from New York

My dear Jane, here the morgues are full.
Our dead have become a logistical nightmare.
Churches closed their doors. Priests offer
Virtual prayers to those who can access the ether.

This morning I am thinking about virtual prayers.
You say there in London you relive your childhood,
World War Two: shortages, community gathering in,
Exchanging words of encouragement.

But here in New York the sick line up along
The avenues, coughing, waiting for the hospitals
Where doctors without protective gear
Must tend to them, no matter what.

One spent 17,000 US dollars on masks
Bought from the black market, the price
Marked up 800 times. In one day he sees
Almost as many patients as there are days in a year.

The thieves hoard lifesaving equipment for profit.
Our president has a little price tag for our parents:
He says the economy *must* be open by Easter,
He says he imagines the churches full of people!

I am reliving the house arrest years, the Cold War,
Then the enemy outside the front door
Had keys to let itself into the house.
Now the enemy is invisible and I can't hear the keys.

Our Governor went on television to demand
Help for the hospitals: "Where are the respirators?"
He said we need 30,000, we have 400.
Our loved ones have become a string of numbers.

It's not all dark, Jane. The robin hops by the front door.
The grass turned green almost overnight,
Our first blue hyacinth bloomed at the back of the house
And the yew stirs with red cardinals and blue jays.

I am going to spend the day contemplating
The meaning of virtual prayer and thinking about virtue.
But I will also cook, clean, and walk with my children,
To feel the real, to protect myself against the imagined.

March 26, 2020

Sitting among the tulips

(Holy Week, 2020)

He writes from my grandparents' house,
His daughter brings her toddler by the front gate
To see the tulips, about one thousand,
Fully grown and ready to unfold.

He says the girl giggles at the sight of flowers,
Names colours, but won't go into the garden
And he won't hold her. He says no one will buy
This Easter, even funerals forego the flowers.

Death all around him is no punishment for sins:
Oh, no. God delivers him warm sunshine and flowers,
Budding trees, the sparrows that have so much talk to do
This season, flying from one coffin to the other.

*

I imagine him standing among tulips, taking note,
Birdsong louder than any he can recall; a glow
Of pink, red, and yellow petals touch his hands
With false reassurance that this too shall pass.

Fields

Orthodox Easter, 2020

In warmer places, where the sun lingers,
Fields offer the first harvest.

The farmer understood light's labour
And the generosity of water:

Snap peas, strawberries, tomatoes,
Squash and green beans gladden the eye.

But this is not the usual season.
This year the farmer buries his harvest.

The tractor calls the crows to feast on
Earth's fruit, crushed in the furrowed field.

*

Miles away the city parking lots are filled
With cars in which families wait for food.

Bird's eye view shows them like toys in rows,
Figures with face masks and gloves

Place a box in each car with food
Flown in from across the border.

No one knows why this is.
The farmer ploughs the food into the soil.

The hungry don't go harvest
The fields, pay what they can.

*

The city streets are lined with trucks
Where hospital workers store the dead,

If each person could be remembered
With a fistful of flowers, the glasshouses

Would empty out. But this is not the time
For old prayers, rituals and incense.

We take away the bodies, following
The protocols for toxic waste.

Our world is sick this season, we're sick
And dying, we plough our harvest in the fields.

*

My mother has kept the Lent as every year
And she has baked sweet bread.

We won't go home for Resurrection.
The priest left the candles in the mailbox.

My father calls me "my little soul," says
They can't tell how this will end,

We recall the parable of the mustard seed,
We know the right time to plant

Is when the fields are ploughed, and
Water from our tears is plentiful.

April

Last night's rain
pelted
the cherry
blossoms.

This morning,
the ground
remembers
snow.

Blue butterfly

the blue butterfly

in the May garden flutters:

dance with me, let's dance!

Language

some climb
on the backs of words
to go places

others carry
words on their backs—
humps on camels

Air and music

Our lilac has bloomed.
All day long birds sing and call,
They are delicate and restless –
Letters hopping from word to word.

*

Words flee one language for another,
They fit like new handles on old doors
Opening and closing the same arguments.
In my country peonies bloom.

May 15, 2020

Morning hours

Seasons crumble into months
filled with loved faces stranded other-where.

The robin hops in the cherry tree,
the cuckoo tests the bark,

the blue jay caws in the blossoms;
they can't stop the clamour in the head.

*

Light moves into corners, the spider blinks
in its web, the book spine is visible.

Here is a day rising from the block of time:
Come, says Alba, see what you can find.

My daughter sits on the threshold
Singing to the birds. She intones vowels,

Orioles send consonants back.
The hour fills with their song.

*

The faces visit throughout the day
Smiling otherworldly as if to say,

You're only imagining this, the skies
Are open, book your flight.

Do not point your gun at a child

Once you were a child too,
And your father must have carried you
On his shoulders, from where
You could look the grown-ups in the eyes.

Do not point your gun at a child
Who holds in her hand a bag of crisps—
Food her only weapon, her father's shoulders
The only vantage point for this world

That burns in flames before her.
People have come to ask for dignity,
This girl must learn it is safe to ask
For a better life, do not point your gun at her.

Once you were a child too
And your father must have carried you
On his shoulders, from where
You could see the world you will live in:

Do not point your gun at this girl
Do not point your gun at her father,
Take off your helmet and look in their eyes
There is a love of life in them you can only see

If you do not point your gun at this girl,
Who is learning at a tender age that no man
Should kneel on the neck of another man,
That no one has the right to take another's life.

June 1, 2020

Stony Brook

At the beginning I loved the quiet. When people began dying by the hundreds and the schools closed, I started counting backwards from fourteen, waiting for symptoms to show up: did I get something while traveling through Penn, on the train back to Long Island, did my husband catch the virus on the flight back from Geneva, did my children…? And on that thought I would stop. What if my children contracted the virus?

We began taking walks around the neighborhood once the warmer weather arrived, counting buds of magnolias, daffodils, and hyacinths. It was so quiet that we took up studying birdsong. My daughter, who is eight, made a Google slideshow about the red cardinals. We played the bird calls on the computer next to the open windows and the birds answered from the trees outside. A woodpecker tapped the tree across the garden. Deer families walked through the backyard as if no one was home.

We baked: focaccia, cakes, flatbreads, whole wheat loaves. We roasted all the veggies we could buy and made platters of colors. I made blackberry-blueberry-raspberry-strawberry compote every single week. And soups, lots of soups. We dressed up and went "out for dinner" in the dining room, at the *Restaurant Chez Maman*. I tried to write. I lectured and preached about the current politics in the kitchen, mostly to clanking pots and pans, while my husband took up residence in our son's bedroom to take the calls from work. Baby rabbits began appearing in the garden, under the butterfly bush. Blue jays landed on rails by the back door and darted off like mini planes when someone stepped close to the windows. People were dying in the thousands and a field hospital went up nearby. When I drifted to sleep, I saw refrigerated trucks in my mind's eye.

I never dreaded the word "heroes" so much. Our leaders and our media slapped that word on the foreheads of health care professionals; the burden of caring for Covid patients without protective equipment was public and made emotional with parades, flyby acrobatics, and sirens. My sister is a nurse. She will never abandon her patients. She called: "Will you raise my girls if we both die?" Her husband is also a nurse. Their doctors were writing their wills too. How strange to have to prepare for dying in the summer of your life. But who could have imagined our new lives six months ago?

We put out the hammock, the badminton net, and the soccer goals. On my fiftieth birthday we danced in the living room, my husband, our children, and I. School is over. On summer solstice we replaced the glass doors with the screen ones and hosed ourselves in the backyard to cool off from the heat. Our flights to Italy were canceled: it will be the second year without seeing our family there. I am trying to remember sitting down with them all, over chilled wine, at Gradara, and then the evening plunge into the sea. Sometimes the connection on Zoom or WhatsApp becomes blurry and I have this strange sense that we are losing each other in the ether. Life is on hold, time keeps rushing through the neighborhood gardens.

July 17, 2020

The Arrow of Time

We are in the backyard
With our children at night
Looking at the stars:

"The light of the Orion Nebula
Began its journey to us
At the time of the Roman Empire."

Time expands, now we live
Fourteen billions years after
The beginning of time.

Space widens and grows
Larger, the space arrow
Follows time's arrow.

Energy, which is heat,
Decreases, it's much colder
Now in the Universe,

"Even on a hot day like this,"
You say. But it's hot
Inside the nebulae—

Those "beds of young stars"
That are cooling down
As they grow into adulthood.

*

And so, since we're star dust,
How can we not embrace
Our temperate onward journey,

The office and the living
Room, their ample space
For each, with time alone?

The marriage is made
Of words and the space
Between each of them.

I search the Orion Nebula
On our wedding anniversary—
Our two young stars grow.

*

Last evening on our walk
We saw a pair of red cardinals
Chase each other on the street.

I couldn't stop thinking
About good omens,
Their loyalty to one another.

A house later, a baby hawk
Attacked a nest of sparrows,
And the tiny birds pecked

At the hawk's wings, cried
Together, coordinated missile
Attacks, one after the other

Till the hawk flew to the top
Of the chimney. When
It returned, it hit the nest

And we left when wings
Flapped in branches,
Saw the mother hawk

Watch the hunt from
The top of the chimney,
Large and glorious.

No matter how small we are,
Fear disappears when it's
Time to protect the nest.

*

There are many things
We see in the quieter world
These days of Lockdown.

Schools of fish ruffle
The sea surface, now that
Few boats disturb the water.

Two monarch butterflies
Circle around us
Outside the front door.

A flock of quails waddles
Through the back garden,
Roses blossom constellations.

Silence feels airy between us.
Time won't retrace itself.
Yet, in your eyes I see

Our past together, one
Single arrow aiming
The way of the stars.

2 August 2020

Laughter
for Stefano

His voice is changing, it breaks
The banks of childhood like a river
Conquering boulders, rushing over.

His laughter tumbles down the stairs
In waterfalls that sometimes bring down
Tree branches, little thunders beautiful to hear.

Yeah, he laughs, and then he laughs again
Straight into my heart, where I keep him
In miniature images, his baby head inside my palm

Those first days when I couldn't tell
How such a tiny being will grow to kiss
My forehead in the mornings, declaring

"Morning of the Excellent" in the kitchen.
How I love the way he sits in my mind's eye,
The boy I look up to, and the tiny, dreamy face,

Working that first smile that so thrilled me,
The milky, drowsy look, and the smart
Clear-eyed boy who takes my hand on walks.

She looks in the mirror
For Alisa

Her lovely head carries all the summer gold
And I follow her from room to room
The way one chases sunlight in winter.

She stops at the mirror and looks at us both
Through the sky of her eyes, which we know
Erupts in storms of tears that clear as quickly

As they arrive. She looks deep enough
Into me that I can read her on my own:
"I want you to see what I see," she says.

The mirror memorizes our faces,
Mine ageing, hers framed by an endless
String of ponytails, pig tails and braids.

*

She sings the hours into a timelessness
Where she invents the music and the words,
The conversations with the birds

Outside the windows, the flock of quails
Traveling through our garden
On their way who knows where—

In this way inventing me too, so now
I am no longer mother but again a child
Seeing things I did not know to look for.

September

The summer's gone like a conversation
slipping out of hearing in the next room.

In the sweltering afternoons, the children
memorized all the world's capitals,

and learned to use the semicolon,
as if still hoping to link one place or season

with another by things which make sense,
or by ways in which one completes the other.

At West Meadow Beach the tides were low,
so we strolled with the horseshoe crabs

far out on sandbanks, where blue crabs walked
sideways, and the water made the far seem near.

Walking among talking leaves
For Alisa

She logged off the virtual school
And we went for a walk on the streets
Talking about the warm weather.

I was saying something about
Ripe sunlight and the smell of leaves,
When the maple to our left began

Uttering what seemed like words,
Its papery, feathery inflections, recalling
Now a flock of birds, now pages turning.

Leaves fell on our shoulders, clinging
To her hair, she giggled in surprise:
The tree was asking for a conversation.

*

There wasn't any wind, yet every tree
We passed by sent off thousands
Of speaking leaves: we opened our arms

Trying to hold their words, and we said
Out-loud our hopes, which we attributed
To those spiriting messengers.

Branches showered us with summer
Golds from the tops, and I took them to be
Angels telling stories, dancing in the air.

The two of us laughed all the way home;
I felt so grateful she believed me, and
Heard with me the talking autumn trees.

This October, winnowing

The day has shortened, hours are
Books between tightened bookends,
Light slants into the under-growth.

The sun places its last kiss on the roses
As insects devour their dying leaves.
And so the summer sighs into fall:

This is the autumn I have no words for.
Apple picking, meals with friends—
Distant memory. Fear gnaws at the heart.

The virus, like a sickness of the conscience
Has spread together with the war among
The righteous. Hope rattles its inflamed lungs.

Justice coughs, kindness wheezes and spits,
Faith plays double game with oath
And governance, truth has lost both legs.

*

I see us dancing in the kitchen years ago,
Salted vine leaves on the wooden board, herbs,
Mother holding house the way the breast-bone

Covers the heart from whatever could strike,
Father calling for the music, "Children, where
Is the cassette?" We were on Helen Street.

There are calls. There is silence during
The calls. There are quiet walks in the garden
After the calls. The virus roams.

The sun has shortened its working hours.
Time pushes its bookends of light closer
Together. Many will not see the winter.

*

We walk around the yew tree. Blue jays
Hide inside tight-wound branches.
The back garden is a busy landing strip.

A cardinal perches on the kitchen rails,
The chipmunk family argues in the gutters
By the stairs, crickets in widened cracks

Sing away the nights in the basement,
As I pace upstairs in the dark kitchen;
A woodpecker knocks on the dormer:

Here is the harvest brought by these
Visiting creatures—memories squirreling
Their freedoms away:

Now I see her, never happy on her own
But glowing whenever we were with her,
I see her taking her smile from our faces.

On this day, we send our love

Thirty-one years ago today,
The other end of the world

Stung as if we were looking
Directly into the sun;

Since then we learned
To look at the sunlit ground.

*

On this day, we send our love
To those who are scaling the wall,

Those who are stepping
On a precarious raft,

Those who are hiding
In the boxes stacked on a truck:

We know it isn't play or malice
That makes you take this road.

On this day, we send our love
And our hope that you will land

As we did, on the verdant earth
Among welcoming people.

The ground has fallen
From under you, we know,

Just like the road vanished
From under our feet.

On this day when we recall
Those first days of freedom,

We send you our love: for
You will need every kind word.

*November 17, 2020, on the anniversary of
my family's immigration to America.*

The Pearl

Who would have known we'd be staying home
Nearly a year, the house growing around us
Like a shell, shutting out the life we knew?

Seasons washed over the roof like tides:
The spring rains, the torrid heat of summer,
These autumn winds snapping off tree limbs,

While impassive fleets of stars reigned
Over the sky wiped clean as a windshield,
Once the planes stood eerily still in hangars.

There were blue moons, and red moons,
Quarters and half-moons, moving from one
Window to another all the sleepless nights

I paced making plans to re-join people,
To embrace and greet, to open the door
For my children's friends coming to play.

Who would have known we'd remain shut in,
Growing nacre-like layers over the world's cries
That entered our lives, and settled there?

Sfintul Neculai

For Grandfather Neculai

It was bitter cold back then
but often there was no snow,

we lit the fire with candle stubs
and grapevine twigs:

who can ever forget
that holy smell of home?

You told us to clean our boots,
not to annoy *bunica* that day:

we obeyed, gifts were on their way—
strawberry-filled candy,

maybe even an orange
wrapped in newspaper.

And then you told us
to go to the kitchen window

to see *Moş Neculai* in the yard
shaking his beard, from which

snow would fall on the ground.
Oh, holy night, twigs of pear tree

In the jar in the kitchen:
Will they blossom by the New Year?

Have we been good enough
to find gifts in boots

on our way to school?
Vine Moșul, fiți cuminți copii.

*

My children don't know
how to conjure up the winter.

Something deep and far back
hankers for snow, but where are you,

Bunicu, who shared the saint's name,
and filled my shoes with so many gifts,

before I vanished into the world
like the grass under the snow?

Christmas

There were many carols,
but they arrived on screen—
from Maramureş.

The four of us put up the tree
which glistened in the sunlight
comforting this winter.

Champagne on zoom
together with our tears;
how this time last year

no one could have imagined
these holidays when we'd fall
silent, not knowing what to say.

Time Being

We did not make these doors,
Yet we too must walk through them.

Truth and Justice swing on rusted hinges,
Vandals bang them on the wall.

There is blood on the marble floor.
Soldiers walk in with their guns

Like schools of fish in the sea,
Choreographing the shape of a monster.

*

The miasma of lies suffocates the air.
The righteous are affected by disaffection.

Newsmakers are tangled in headlines,
Isms rhyme with schisms.

We did not build these doors
But we must walk through them

To the other side: where Androcles
Stands with the lion at his feet.

On the 2021 Presidential Inauguration

We must begin with an act of trust,
Even if it is born in the pillaged room,
Where lawmakers kneel behind their desks
As the mob tramples the law.

From the senators' papers
That bear the prints of vandals' shoes,
From the shards of shattered windows,
From pepper sprayed in policemen's eyes

And from my daughter's screams—
"Mommy, are we going to die?"—
From this destruction trust must emerge
And be placed in a better life.

*

Every farmer knows the soil
Will not yield a perennial harvest
From a single planting, and the yield
Of one harvest is a blessing of care.

The bread on the table will not
Knead itself. It takes all day
To keep an orderly house:
Mothers always have known this.

The thinker understands that ideas
Must suffer countless revisions
If they are to stand the test of time:
Not all revolutions begin the same.

The believer has learned that gratitude,
Which is invisible, immeasurable,
And is born of a willingness to love,
Is the strongest bond we share.

*

From my child's stunned tears,
From the admission that too often
All of us got it all wrong, we must
Begin again to trust – and go on.

Aero garden

A light bulb, water, nutrients
from a small plastic bottle:

basil, dill, and parsley
grow out of paper-rimmed cups

bright green, fragrant
on the kitchen counter.

There is no torrential
summer rain, the ant, the bee,

the squirrel or the bird –
a garden family in sunlight.

And us this year: raising
children in the glow of screens

living rooms in ether,
birthdays on FaceTime,

away from predators
and dust, safe in our chairs

forgetting our nature,
losing our senses,

like these herbs, real
and no herbs at all.

February 2021

Winter cardinal

snow brings cursive tree
writing in relief; red ink
wings correct the text

Anniversary of the heart

For my mother

I remember how time stopped
while the surgeon scraped
the hardness off your heart walls.

One year ago, this week,
I was flying to be with you
so that you'll know

in your heart that I was there
during the slippery hours,
hoping to make light of it,

and take you home
to kitchen and the dog
and the daily goings on.

A whole year has gone by
without seeing you
in flesh and blood.

Time has calcified
like the deposits in the heart,
pushing the valve to limit.

Morning in the garden

I

Today's sky glows in the distance
like a child waking up from restful sleep,
the snow on tree crowns has a rosy hue.
Now the sun is changing ink as I walk
from room to room, looking
through curtains; the bright light
of day turns the shovelled road to silver,
making mountains out of mounds.
Overnight, the snow on the cherry tree
grew into round petals, opaline almost.

II

A cardinal, blood red, royal,
sings at the very top of the pitch pine,
the melody unfurls in the pure air,
reaches to the roofs of houses
warm under the snow, down
to the opened window, where I stand
to receive his ancient, thrilling language
that sounds me through and through.
The cardinal's song is now a river,
the ice film on the maple trees glistens.

III

This winter the snow in the garden
rises like soft bread dough.
Out there in the city a cellist plays
her instrument in a shop window,
a violinist tunes her violin in another;
ambulances wail, life seeps out past
canisters of air, adrenaline injected in the heart,
the intravenous needles meant to rescue
that one final breath. How does the world go on,
how will it live past this gruesome year
of death that stamped its syllable on us,
who receive the music through thick glass?

*February 8, 2021, written on the one-year
anniversary of the first deaths from Covid.*

A promise
For my mother

There have been strange visitations
You felt only now and then, when
The dog lay in the middle of the road
Refusing to walk, sensing you about to faint;

Or when you got up from the table
And the house moved with you
As if on a merry-go-round, the porcelain
Spinning in a brief, silent film.

Someone read the map of your brain
And found there ravaged side-roads:
"Interval development of subcortical infarct,
Of the upper left frontal operculum, chronic now."

"Operculum" is a lid, *acoperire*—the word
Protects our vulnerable language, itself in need
Of sheltering by something less brittle.
Your new hair colour looks lovely!

Wait until I get there, please, stay till
I can come to hold you and talk about cures;
Now the roads are blocked, a virus stalks and kills,
People fall like grapes from vines. I'll be there.

Waiting for spring

Under the last of the snow the trees
Wiggle their roots; the warming sieve
Awakens branches and their twigs
That stood numb with cold for months.

Last evening before supper
Half a dozen young deer galloped
Through the yard, their sound
A surprising stampede of happiness.

Booming birdsong, as if the hearing
Itself has sharpened in our bodies,
And windows are raised, doors flung open,
Our eyes train on imagining new buds.

But it is fraught, all is fraught this spring
When the mind rushes everything in
To offer consolation: when the blue jay
Is perceived to have arrived to cheer us up.

We have not left the island in one year,
No one has crossed our threshold,
We remained closed in, in the house,
The way the trees seem dead in winter.

Half a million dead: who can count on
The accuracy of the number?
The earth groans with the cadavers of those
Who last year went about their worries

With notepads filled with things to do,
Bills to pay, families to feed—
Just when the world came to a halt.

25 February 2021

PART III

E quindi uscimmo a riveder le stelle.

(And there we emerged to see again the stars.)

—Dante, *Inferno*,
Canto XXXIV line 139

First of March

The snow across the yard rises
In white drifts under trees, breath of earth;
The low fog taller than the children,
Who sing like trilling robins

In the middle of a late snowstorm.
The thrills and dangers of spring chills
Give way to irrepressible possibility—
Burgeoning buds, crocuses under snow.

What now? Time to plot the garden,
Dream the summer feasts of sweet peas
And tomatoes, watermelons, strawberries
Growing in the song of orioles.

The tree doctor

Ms. Carmen, he smiled, I'll make you a nice garden
But first we must take care of the trees, cut off dead limbs.
So here he is this afternoon, with an orange rope
Fastened around his body, climbing
To the top branch that arches over the house.

He greets the trunk as he would a close friend,
Makes his way up, one boot and one glove at a time,
Chainsaw behind his back, the bark responding
To his body with dry, reassuring sound, while I
Stand in the yard with my children, holding my breath.

Then he cuts off the branches we feared this past year –
Precisely, like a surgeon, one by one; and they fall
With a loud thump to the ground, sending little tremors
Under our feet. I watch him transfixed: he is agile,
Entrancing like a dancer in the tree's embrace.

When he appears on the ground, down from the treetop,
He asks, are these your children, they are so young,
Then he turns directly to my face, smiling once again:
You waited for a long time to have children. Yes,
I started late, I say, feeling myself tree and branch at once.

11 March 2021

Hawk

He is not afraid of this wind
That seems to move the air around
Like a pair of hands, and turns
My blue tablecloth into a sail.

He appears directly above me
Straight from the midday sun, swoops
Into the backyard with a war-cry,
His shadow darkening the grass.

How he plays into the thermals,
How he strides the currents! Blinding
Sunrays through his wings, it seems
As if he wears a cloak of godly fire.

He decelerates with exhilarating ease,
Turns above the chimney, so close to me,
The sun stings my eyes full of him,
But when I can see again, he is not there.

31 March 2021

Nest of songs

I want to nestle you in the songs of orioles,
Weaving mating calls across the maples
Their voices concolorous, suasive,
Wheedling leaves from enchanted trees.

This house withstood the test of isolation
Four seasons and one more
With just some paint peeling off the walls,
But not you; you whittled in silence
With the wall of one sentence: "I do not know."

Yet, here we are, above the ground,
Suspended between spring songs tangling
In air all around the garden and the streets,
Palms of the magnolia opening to say, "Hold this."

31 March 2021

Daffodils

It's
almost
Easter.
This
Holy Week
the daffodils
light up
like candles
in the sand trays
at the altar.
The cardinals'
joyful
whistling
braids
the two worlds.
The crocus cups
are filled
for communion.

2 April 2021

Mourning Dove eggshell

Mourning doves nest everywhere here,
I know them by their longing songs
Turning the midday into a thought
About being otherwhere in feelings,

Or up there, in the mind of questions
Of how the two of us and our children
Could settle in one place or another,
Where we would somehow feel at ease.

The same cooing music brings me back
To the ground though, and settles me
Like the voice of someone I love
Calling my name for reassurance

That I am still around, within reach.
This Easter Saturday the doves left
A glossy white, half-shell in my path
Outside the kitchen door, in the grass:

An offering of news that their chicks
Now hatched around the garden.
I took it for a scattered petal of magnolia
At first, a wind whim, but in my hand

I saw it: a hint of happiness unseen.
I turned the eggshell over in my palms
To our children's mellifluous ahhs and oohs,
Read signs from doves in their smiles.

Easter 2021

Love poem

Somewhere
in the depths of dreams,
the sea calls.
Sea on a clear day
that lets you see
to the bottom of it.
I am told out, I am quiet now.
My head is in your hands.

Irenicon

I fear that what it was, was spent,
We can no longer find ourselves
Or space for each other.

I threw thousands of aster seeds
Around the mailbox, where we go
Every day to look for other news.

I said we need to enclose the space
With stones, so that the lawn mowers
Won't kill the flowers before they grow.

So there you are with our daughter,
Digging stones around the backyard
And building a circle around the seeds;

Busy with something to do,
Designing the shelter for what we
Could be seeing months from now,

An address to what will become memory,
A way to address each other, marking
That which could grow inside us.

23 April 2021

First of May
For Kathy

> Io retornai da la santissima onda
> rifatto sì come piante novelle
>
> rinovellate di novella fronda,
> puro e disposto a salire a le stelle.
> —Dante, *Purgatorio*, Canto XXXIII 140–145

One week of furious flowering, when forsythia
burns in gardens, magnolias open like butterflies,
the ground fills with blue wild pansies, violets,
and then the winds come stealing all the petals
with their scented spells: the grass, a meadow
of rhododendron blooms early in the morning,
the edges of the garden, coloured. Spring
is passing once again, leaving chicks in nests,
us outside planting just as lilacs begin to bloom,
and summer shade of maples leafing.

I try to hold my thoughts to all these images
while I lift fresh curtains up to hang on windows,
where light will pass through, sheltering the eyes
from too much sun but letting them also see outside,
where forsythia changes from yellow to green.
The Orthodox Easter Lent at the end,
praying with my children over new seeds we planted
and the robins blessed with their songs,
I emerged from the holiest waves
restored even as new trees were
renewed with new leaves,
pure and prepared to rise to the stars. *

*my translation of the Dante's verses quoted in the epigraph

PART IV

kai kunteron allon pot' etla

(you have survived worse things)

—Homer

Change is Afoot

What we called "us" shattered
Like a glass vase filled with
Seashells and rosy stones collected
Over many years from seashores,
Ocean shores, lakeshores,
Wide and narrow beaches—with
So much care, sharing each find,
First alone, and then with children.

Tenses are changing, time grows
Distant and cold. I am unsure
About rescuing the riches from
The shards of glass, the hours that pass
With palpable weight in them.
The peony is taking root by the mailbox
In the middle of the unsprouted asters.
The marigold lamps hold steady.

Change is afoot. Words follow
A changed course. The storm in the kitchen
Over frozen bread no one has wanted
Since Christmas: I have been baking
Almost every day for much more than a year,
There is warm bread on the table now.
Have I saved enough of what was "us"
In words, for memory's sake?

20 May 2021, Stony Brook

Pollen rains

With the green-golden dust
that settles on the windowsills
before the Saturday cleaning,
come the butterfly-like petals
landing on our shirts, between
white strawberry flowers,
piles of soft pink under trees.

The air is thick. Trees drop
caterpillars on the road, blue
half-shells of robins' eggs.
Before the end of June
the house will be coated
in pollen dust, our windows
will need washing, windowpanes
will be green as moss.

I go out with the children
in the pollen rains,
we are doused in them,
stained and sneezing,
watery-eyed, thrilled.
At the end of June we will
leave you pacing in the house
in the dark room, we will drive
away in the gray morning,
pollen dust on the car windshield.

May 22, 2021

Conversation with the soul

In the night the moon traveled closer to the perigee;
moon and sun aligned hour by hour in precise
positions on opposite ends of the turning earth –
I watched the disappearance of the moon in the making:
before sundown I will see both eclipse and super blood moon,
witness disappearance of light and light that fills the night.
Light is not a trick, it lets you see the shape of things.

*

The soul says husband and wife are holy names, their duties sacred;
marriage is the earth in conversation with the sun and the moon.
When the room fills with pacing, anger building up
like stores of dynamite, and when bile spills over the dishes
laid on the table, I taste the bitter days, says the soul.

*

I made a map of the places where you look:
it's almost always a net from floor to children's faces,
the chair to your right, the chair to your left, the plate,
the sink, the office desk, the basement door, TV,
a hole in the space I occupy at the table in the kitchen,
holes in the map where I walk around rooms –
a traffic of detours from rooms, where
I happen to step in by mistake, unnoticed.

The space where you look
is a fabric filled with the places where I am
marked as absent; light and air come in,

your eyes hold nothing at all – a shred
of a map of insistence on my non-presence.
The same map can be made
of conversations that take place around
and without me, the air itself unevenly filled
with words precisely directed to kill
the heart of love. Husband and wife are eclipsed
by turns on the opposite ends of marriage
light showing only the injured faces.

25–29 May 2021

Their first strawberry

They go to the garden several times a day
To check on the tiniest shoots of lemon balm,
The holy basil, rosemary, thyme, the tomato
Plants that now are sending forth first flowers,
And they see how their strawberries grow,
The first one, blushing: yesterday's pink, ripe now.

I have never seen more happiness in them.
Brother and sister kneel by the bush
To take the fruit of their labor from its stem:
Her nine-year-old hands, his fourteen-year-old
Wise smile, somehow holding her and their garden
In that mysterious glow that tells me they
Will be all right through these fractured days
When parents weep and let go of each other,
And when I see plainly how only half
Of the garden I have planted fifteen years ago
Has taken root and bears the first taste of harvest.

6 June 2021

Whitsun

Again, awake at the first calling of birds
And now the sun pours a golden light
Over the garden and the grass that all night
Were soaked in rain. The orioles and robins,
The doves and tiny sparrows sing in tongues:
Rusaliile, Rusaliile, the descent of the Holy Spirit,
And I pray again in my mother tongue
Lumineaza Doamne mintea mea, bring light
Into my mind this day, my birthday,
Bring some words that have the force of baptism,
To raise this crumbled marriage back to faith,
When love means trust and trust is the house
Where these two beautiful children of ours grow.

Rusalii, Rusalii, Duminica Rusaliilor,
I am a child again barefoot in the Sunday
Yard of my grandparents, preparing for church,
Washing my face with water from a tin cup.
The coming of wisdom is celebrated today,
I try to sense it in the songs of orioles, the joyful
Calling of the cardinals and mourning doves
That won't let up, and hold me up, feeling
The gentle breath of God – the morning air
Through the open windows – that moves
Over the faces of my sleeping children, who
Went to bed praying the madness in the house will end.
The sun stands still, waits for our hearts to change.

20 June 2021, Stony Brook

Crossing the Sound

Now that all the words are said
And we find ourselves searching beyond
The point of no return, I walk
Through the garden. The baby roses
Are up to my waist, but they are dying
From disease or parasites, or both.
The butterfly bush thrives – grown the height
Of our daughter – and the tips are purple,
Preparing to bloom. The wildflowers surprise us
With things new – red and white poppies,
Pink forget-me-nots, purple silky skirts of
One flower I can't quite name.

Seven more days and I will cross the Sound
With our son and daughter, leave the strawberries
And tomatoes behind, the black-eyed Susans
By the office window, the hanging pots
With colorful petunias. I'll have the post stopped
And held at the Post-Office for the summer.
You will fly across the ocean alone
Taking with you the pacing and the sighing,
The calculated stinging looks, the timed
Silences and the unanswered questions.
I am alert, lucid, and prepared for the ferry,
The end of love is always clear-headed.

Stony Brook, 18 June 2021

Don't lose heart

Here's the end of June like a messenger
Wet from rain and tired from the road.

I wept with relief on the ferry, car secured
At the bottom, children up on the deck with me

Masks on, disinfectant in hand, hot chocolate
That to them was too perfect and sweet

After the morning that was tied in the knot
Of grief. The water was covered with fog

But the ferry went straight through and
We set the course for the journey on the other side.

North of Bridgeport, the rain washed the windshield
And by the time we crossed the Appalachians

The sun of our first day of freedom shone through.
Our road cut through green forests, swung around

Mountains and hills, into sunshine, to Buffalo
Where we panicked in the hotel room just

As it began to rain again. It was a night we couldn't
Wait to end, so we waited for the morning at the window.

II

Don't lose heart I told the children on our way
To Michigan, don't lose heart, we must be strong.

The skies cleared past Erie, where the lake appeared
Like a blue ribbon that stretched to Cleveland

Where the planes took off above the highway.
When we arrived in Michigan and the landscape

Changed to the green of forests, the road lined
With pink and yellow flowers, we turned our thoughts

To the family awaiting us, to their gardens, and
All the time we spent without them. We put away

The masks, closed the disinfectants, decided
This will be the time for kisses and for hugs.

This place is healing, my son said as we walked
Through my sister's garden – zucchini flowers yellow

And large, delicate and strong, the fragrant bed of thyme,
The lettuce patch, tall tomato bushes, climbing peas.

Three cats around the hilly garden, roosters, hens,
Guinea fowl, and a family of ducks were talking

All at the same time. I stood among the plants
And felt my sister's love in there.

I can feel freedom here, my son said, the place teems
With life, come play with the cats! In the house

The table was laid with food for celebration,
Chilled champagne. I want to hug the family

And the whole world, my daughter said,
It's been so sad for us the past few months

I feel white spots of emptiness inside.
Here we are, I said, go get the hugs, my love.

III

We are now at my parents' house, where the lilies
Have bloomed, the asters and petunias sing their

Colors, Remi the dog nuzzles the children
And their *bunica* awaits with their favorite food.

It's the last day of June. Last night we talked
About the turn our lives must take from now on.

Don't lose your hearts, my father said, you will
Go on, you must stay strong. You have this house

My mother said, from the beginning this has
Been your refuge, you are not alone, let's celebrate

Your safe journey here. After you rest, we go
To visit the Sleeping Bear Dunes, the Pictured Rocks

Don't lose your heart, you must go on with
Everything you've got, leave the self-doubt behind.

30 June 2021

Up North

I. To the Sleeping Bear Dunes

We left on my mother's birthday by way
Of Ludington, where memories played
Their tricks of bringing back the first freed self,
And then the two of us starting a family.
The children talked in the car about the trip ahead.

In the middle of the Manistee National Forest
The connection was lost and when you took us
By surprise with the call, your voice and our voices
Took turns trying to reach across blank spaces
As you pretended that nothing terrible had happened.

Up on the hills of M22, our broken souls were
Greeted by the bluest water, sparkling with the breath
Of God: it emerged on the side of the serpentine road,
The roadside lookout where we climbed the wooden steps
Above the tree line, kissed by the sweetest wind.

Out there on the horizon, farther north, is where
We'd see the momma bear and her cubs
Who are now islands. So we drove through maples
And pines, past Crystal Lake, all the way
Till the signpost I've searched for, thrilled me.

II. Traverse City Bay

The words between us this morning cannot build
A bridge that anyone can cross, and we all know it,

Even as I try to explain that no repair can take place
On cellular phone calls from across the ocean
When trust was breached, the foundations shaken.

The children and I ask for economy of words:
A silent summer with a promise to reflect.
We stand looking through the windows at the still bay
Our own faces looking back at us from the glass
As we explain to you that we want to see your face

If we are to build a bridge that can withstand this pain.
To one another we seem readable, within ourselves
There are inscrutable griefs: if we see things in this light,
Then the inside and the outside change places,
And one can't tell where the words come from.

What if the source of words remains a mystery
And if the hidden becomes readable, in a large
Script in clear light, and what seemed plain is inscrutable?
Who, then, can trust the art of making oneself understood,
How does one know the step backwards is not forward?

III. Dune Climb

Here they are, arms in the air,
Helping their grandma up the dune
Laughing and shouting in the wind,
Their faces, as children's faces should be,
Finally released from griefs.

The horizon seems so close, we trick
Ourselves that we can touch the sky,
All the way till we reach the top and see it

Jump over to the next golden dune that takes
Forever to climb, and only minutes to descend.

Later in the evening a storm will
Whiten the bay and turn sky and lake
Into mirages that will vanish and reappear
Between clouds, our faces at sunset
Borrowing light from a fiery glow.

IV. Two Peninsulas

The first drive is on the outer edge of land – *finis terre*
With vineyards and the lighthouse with the tree roots
Still growing in the water. Sutton Bay and Northport
With their thousands of flowers and boats, the tiny
Airport with tiny planes, the yellow and the red house,
The gas station where we play the lottery and win back
The price of the tickets to my mom's delight.

But the second peninsula with the cherry orchards
Grabs our hearts – the children make a first memory,
I am replaying mine as we touch the cherries
On the branches, buy loads of them to taste the yellow,
And the slightly bitter dark red, the sour light-red flesh.
Hawks glide along the rolling hills, the sun prepares to set,

But not yet. There is still time for the drive along the edges,
By the water. Time to reach the 45th parallel at the lighthouse.
Time to walk through the woods, look at the water again,
To realize that father, mother, and children are creatures
Of the space halfway between the North Pole and the Equator,
That we never strayed too far from this longitude.

V. Mackinac Bridge

It's green, and they call it the miracle bridge
Because it can withstand the greatest winds,
It has the longest length on the northern hemisphere,

And its pylons are planted at great depths:
Now that's a bridge that will carry us across
What is to come. This is where I must return to live.

Imagine words rooted in dangerous depths,
Extended across enough miles they seem unlikely
To reach shore to shore, designed to bend in tempestuous

Winds just enough to bear the pressure, unbreakable,
Reliable, and so beautiful, they make a work of art
As they sustain, give access, help us carry on.

VI. Up North

We enter Hawatha National Forest west of St Ignace
And do not leave it till we reach the shores of Lake Superior,
Which is the purest blue, the deepest of the Great Lakes,
And the coldest. The children and I enjoy the silence

We have asked for. In this silence, beyond Munising,
We have the Pictured Rocks, caves of blue, green, red,
And white stone – all rainbow-like – at the edges
Of the water, beautiful as a morning prayer.

Smoked white fish, calligraphy of trees and water,
The bluest, most perfect sky, woods so green

They seem painted. And us, talking in the car, making
Recordings of these days where we'll return for strength.

I tell my children this is our passage to the next
Part of our lives, I insist on a record of it so that
We will turn to it for what it is, not for what we will
Remember through second thoughts, or fog of time.

VII. A sort of celebration

The ferry captain says to cover our ears,
He'll sound the horn, but we are keen on the noise,
So the call to the crossing sounds straight through us.

Arch Rock, white cedar, a terrace restaurant
At the edge of water, flowers overrunning the island,
And dreams, so many dreams of what will happen next

In our lives as the children and I ferry on.
There will always be disappointments about what
We think waits for us, but we are focused

On the journey there, because it reveals things,
Possibilities: in the detours, sights left unseen,
Surprises along the way. Our boat sails through.

July 5–July 12, 2021

They discovered the singing sands

There are times when the moisture between the grains of sand
builds up so precisely, it is possible to make a sort of music
when walking near water's edge, the pressure of each step
setting off a song – its rhythm light or heavy, as the mind
weights down the body, closer to the earth. Summer without you.

She shouts behind me, "Mommy, listen! Listen to the sand!"
But I am already inside the granular melody unfolding
with every step I take, the orchestra of waves and wind
accompanying the hesitance of distance from the water's edge
to the storm beach, where fallen branches and dead monarchs lie.

Through the blowdown, the dune looks eaten in. The jaws of wind
tore through the forest, leaving a layer of exposed roots
like nerve synapses connecting the seen with the unseen, the secret
of dying revealed to the tenderest shoots, embraced by waves,
soothed by changing light, tonight the sun a ball of fire.

I walk in the darkness between my son and daughter, holding hands.
We follow the path by the glow of the round moon. At two in the morning
there is a sky filled with stars above beech, hemlocks, and oaks, and
though we can't tell which is which, we recite the names of trees: white pines,
black cherry and birch, cotton wood, as if they're family around the hearth.

II

I brought them here to hear with me the singing sands,
it's we who make the song with our walking, or else the sand
is silent to our ears – unless we walk with others, hearing them.

This is a gathering place. Here I first knew myself with dreams that could reach to the end of the land and grow in water.

Whatever strength we need to take with us must come
from sleeping on the welcoming earth, on these resilient
dunes filled with music unfolding like a map.
A new journey begins with this summer alone. The loss of you
brought saplings in ravaged forests, singing sands.

29 July 2021

Yvoire—a memory

I remember today, for no good reason
The lost wedding ring you bought in Chicago
At Tiffany's: that sweltering summer
When we married in the rundown garden
Of the village hall, happy as larks.

Gettysburg

Late Sunday afternoon when Michigan
Disappears behind us, my mother and brother
Travel with us halfway home: a trip to Gettysburg –
Words at the end of the battle, the story
Of Pickett's charge my brother tells my children.

Monday morning the sun is red like a painting
In the Pennsylvania sky and I abandon
The straight road, I turn to cross the Blue Ridge
Mountains, where we refill the tank aided
By a man with one arm. A cart and a horse.
Thin serpentines.

Three days of battle history, observation posts,
Oppressive heat, and a hotel with a Civil War canon
In the lobby. My brother explains while we walk
Through the wheatfield, the peach orchard,
Cross the railway line – overgrown and picturesque.
But all I see are the private wars that rage inside of me.

*

A last detour up the Hudson River and the forests of Connecticut
And there we are at the ferry, where another end begins.

8–12 August 2021

The hook
For Alessandro

Still sea, stilled in the morning heat,
Limpid sky with nimbus building up
Somewhere between the cardinal directions
And the water, clean as a lens.

I walked slowly through the receding tide
Ahead of you, since we stopped walking
Together a long time ago. Long enough
That now my mind rejoices in the moment.

There it was—a fish with bluish fins
Trapped by a hook and forgotten there
Together with the hook, dying in pain
While the horseshoe crab walked by.

By the time you caught up with me
I saw it was still moving and I saw
The hook in its mouth. The summer
Of separation must have been like my hand

Pulling the hook very gently out
Of the mouth of the fish, you,
Barely convinced to keep it still, so that
I could work out that last twist of wire:

Its mouth open and trusting, its eyes wide,
Understanding my touch and the shape of hook.
I was distanced, focused only on
Seeing the fish back in the deeper water.

You were stunned holding its body
In our daughter's t-shirt, unknowing,
Unknowable, even as I coaxed it and it
Swam alive, and free, disappearing while

I looked up at the faces of the children,
Trying to explain how it started a second life;
The fish nowhere to be seen, and you:
Left with the hook and the line in your hands.

August 14, 2021

www.ingramcontent.com/pod-product-compliance
Lightning Source LLC
Chambersburg PA
CBHW031637160426
43196CB00006B/458